MEDUSA

MEDUSA

Medusa is so scary! She has skin like dragon scales, bronze hands, golden wings, sharp teeth, and snakes for hair! When she gets angry she sticks out her forked tongue and the snakes wriggle wildly on her head! HISS! It's hard to believe, but Medusa was once a beautiful girl who was admired by all. But now no one goes near her. Everyone is afraid of her because her eyes have the power to turn anyone who dares to look at her into stone. She lives with her sisters, the Gorgons, in a dark forest, far away from everything and everyone.

PERSEUS

The young hero is the son of Princess Danae and the mighty Zeus, king of Heaven and Earth. When he was an infant, he was taken from his homeland by his grandfather Acrisius, king of Argos, and sailed for days locked in a chest with his mother. The sea's waves rocked him, and the calls of the seagulls were his lullaby. Fortunately, a fisherman found the chest, and Danae and baby Perseus jumped out, safe and sound! Now that he is grown up, he's not afraid of anything and is always ready for adventure.

AN ENTRANCING GAZE

Who is that beautiful girl with long black hair? It's Medusa! Her eyes sparkle like emeralds, and everyone falls in love with her at first sight.

Medusa lives happily with her sisters, Euryale and Stheno, and can't wait to get married. Which lucky person will she choose?

One terrible day the young woman accidentally offends the goddess Athena. Poor Medusa! Enraged, the goddess turns her into a frightening creature in the blink of an eye! Oh no!

IN THE LAND OF DARKNESS

Even her sisters are transformed into horrible monsters. The three Gorgons (this is what they are called from then on) flee and hide in a faraway country, in a forest where darkness reigns. Poor Medusa suffers an atrocious fate; she looks terrifying, with scary snakes waving ceaselessly on top of her head, and no one dares to approach her for fear of being turned to stone by her gaze! Her name alone is enough to make people tremble...

THE CHALLENGE

The royal palace is celebrating. King Polydectes wants to get married.

"I'll give you a white horse!" says one of the guests.

"And I a black one as fast as the wind," cries another.

But the young hero Perseus silences everyone: "I will bring you Medusa's head."

AAARGH!

Even the bravest cry out in fright! Medusa is too dangerous. Will Perseus be able to defeat her? Fortunately, there is someone who has heard everything and runs to help him.

A PROTECTIVE SHIELD

It's Athena! The goddess is wise and cunning, and knows Medusa well. No wonder—she was the one who turned her into a horrible monster! She hands Perseus a shield as shiny as a mirror. Perseus is very curious. What's it for?

"Be careful," Athena warns. "You must never look Medusa in the eyes." She explains that he will be able to fight the Gorgon by looking at her reflection in the shiny surface of the shield. Perseus will be able to see Medusa without being turned to stone. He will simply have to walk backward! WOW!

HERE IS HERMES!

What is that tiny shape speeding down from the sky? It gets bigger and bigger and...OH!

Hermes, messenger of the gods, arrives like lightning. On his feet he wears winged sandals, which is why he flies faster than the wind.

"I want to help you too," says Hermes.

Perseus jumps for joy. With the help of the gods, defeating Medusa will be a piece of cake, won't it? The hero scratches his head worriedly.

MAGICAL GIFTS

Medusa lives in a faraway place. How long will it take to get there? And how will Perseus transport her head to King Polydectes's palace?

"You need three very special items," says Hermes. And here they are! A pair of winged sandals just like his own so that Perseus will arrive at his destination in no time. Next is a magic bag in which Medusa's head will be safe. And last is the helmet of the god Hades, which will make our hero invisible!

ON THE WINGS OF THE WIND

Perseus quickly puts on his sandals, takes Hermes's gifts, and is finally ready to go!

AND, WOOSH…

The sandals' wings flap faster and faster, and Perseus soars into the air. Do you think he's scared? No way!

Athena and Hermes are with him. What an outstanding team!

Together they fly over the sea until the sky grows darker and the sun no longer shines. "Land!" cries Perseus suddenly. Below is a strange forest thick with trees. Quickly, they must go down!

MEDUSA!

Perseus looks around, and Hermes and Athena also keep careful watch.

The forest is cold. BRRR!

It's foggy and dark, and there are statues everywhere: squirrels, foxes, deer. These are the animals Medusa has turned to stone with her terrible gaze! There are also many young heroes, turned to stone with their swords drawn. They came all this way to defeat Medusa, just like Perseus.

They are surrounded by a great silence. But where is the monster? Perseus moves a branch aside and...

There is Medusa! She is terrifying.
BOOM BOOM.
Perseus's heart beats like a drum.

Fortunately, the monster is sleeping under a tree, her golden wings folded over her body and sharp teeth protruding from her mouth. The snakes are also asleep, snoring as they coil around her head.

Athena approaches Perseus. "If Medusa opens her eyes, do not look at her!" she reminds him. So he turns around and walks backward, looking at Medusa in the shield's reflection.

THE BIRTH OF PEGASUS...

Suddenly Medusa opens an eyelid. Perseus must be quick: If she wakes up, there will be trouble. Athena guides Perseus's hand and CHOP!
   With a decisive blow he cuts the monster's head off. But what's happening now? Two ears sprout from Medusa's neck, then a milk-white mane, and an instant later...two beautiful wings. "It's Pegasus, the winged horse!" says Hermes.
   Pegasus leaps out and CLIP CLOP!
   He stomps his hooves on the ground in greeting.

... AND CHRYSAOR

The horse shakes his head and snorts. Then he opens his big wings and off he goes! He flies free across the sky.

Perseus watches, spellbound, as Pegasus twirls through the clouds. He doesn't notice that something else is emerging from Medusa's neck. It's a giant! He's huge and clutches a golden sword in his hand.

"Watch out for the giant Chrysaor!" cries Hermes.

All this commotion wakes up Medusa's sisters. They are as frightening as she is, and they are very angry.

GRRR!

MISSION ACCOMPLISHED

Perseus hides his eyes with his hand and puts Medusa's head in the magic bag. Then he wears the invisibility helmet and… POOF!

Chrysaor and the Gorgons look around in amazement, but everyone has disappeared!

"Quick, slip on your winged sandals," says Athena. Perseus flies off just in time, but the bag is very heavy, so Hermes helps him.

Medusa's head is still magical; when Perseus lays the bag down on seaweed to rest, the seaweed turns into corals!

POLYDECTES'S PALACE

Home at last! After a long journey Perseus finally arrives at Polydectes's palace and, after thanking Hermes and Athena, he enters with his gift for the king.

SNIFF SNIFF...

What's that smell? Wafting out of the great hall is the aroma of roasted chicken and freshly baked cakes and bread. Polydectes is at the table, feasting with his friends.

Perseus climbs onto a stool and lifts up the magic bag.

"Here is Medusa's head!" he cries happily.

BULLIES TURNED TO STONE

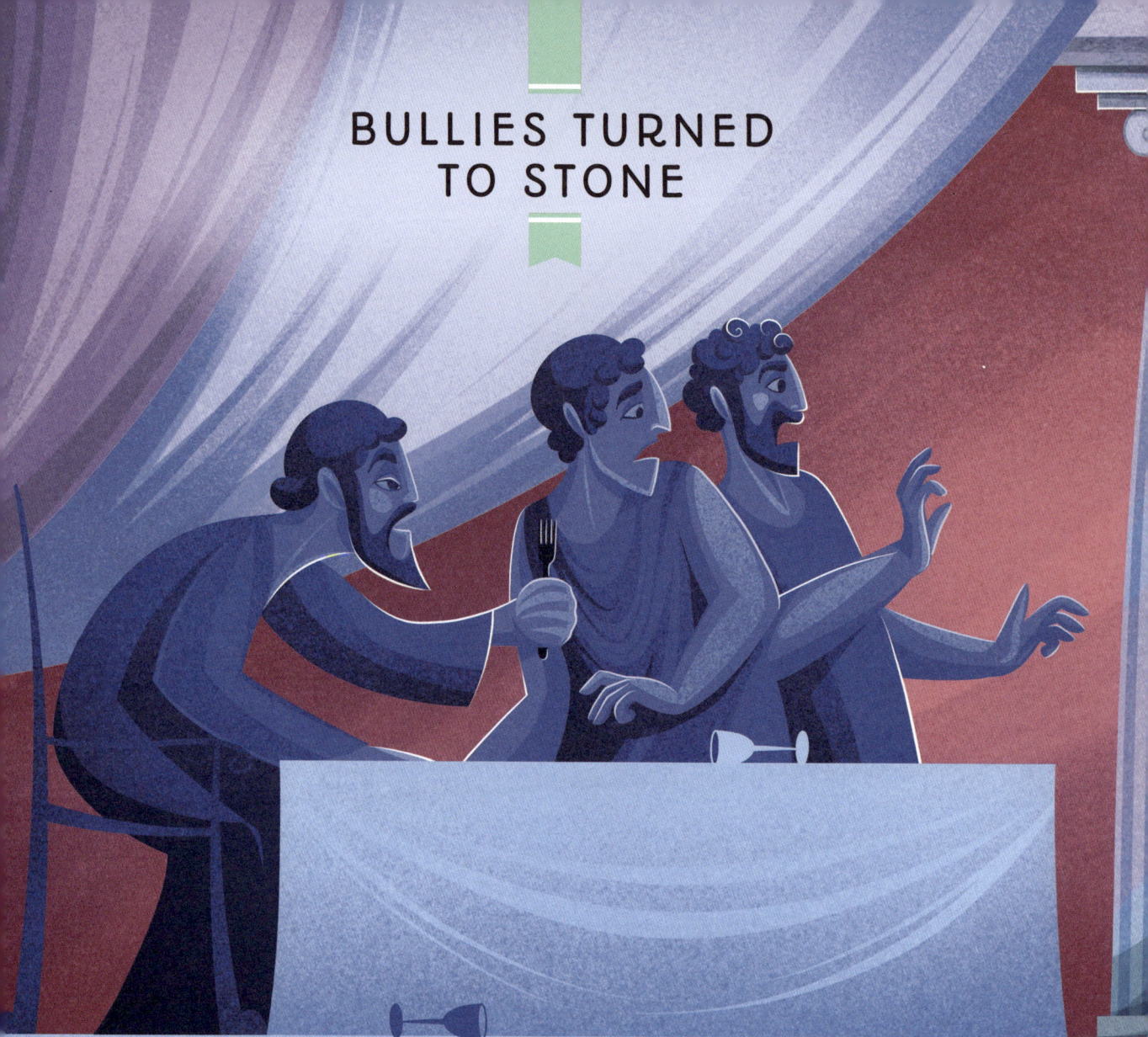

But instead of applauding, everyone jumps to their feet in terror.

"What kind of joke is this?"

"Go away!"

"Get out of here!"

Some shout, some raise their fists, some draw their swords.

They pick on Perseus and say a lot of mean words to him....

King Polydectes is the most frightened and calls his guards, ordering them to put Perseus in prison. So Perseus pulls out Medusa's head and... WOW!

In a split second, he turns all those bullies into statues. Justice is served!

Sonia Elisabetta Corvaglia

Sonia Elisabetta Corvaglia was born in the province of Lecce, Italy, and currently lives and works in Milan. She teaches high school literature and collaborates with local libraries as a consultant for projects and workshops to promote literacy and reading. She also oversees school programs to encourage inclusivity and combat bullying, including cyberbullying. Corvaglia has authored and ghostwritten numerous novels, children's books, and online articles.

Anna Láng

Anna Láng is a Hungarian graphic designer and illustrator who is currently living and working in Sardinia. After attending the Hungarian University of Fine Arts in Budapest, she graduated as a graphic designer in 2011. She was employed for three years at an advertising agency, at the same time working with the National Theatre of Budapest. In 2013, she won the award of the city of Békéscsaba at the Hungarian Biennale of Graphic Design for her Shakespeare poster series. At present, she is working passionately on illustrations for children's books. In recent years she has brilliantly illustrated a number of titles for White Star Kids.

White Star Kids™ is a trademark of White Star s.r.l.

© 2023 White Star s.r.l.
Piazzale Luigi Cadorna, 6 - 20123 Milan, Italy
www.whitestar.it

Translation: Stephanie Williamson
Editing: Michele Suchomel-Casey

All rights reserved. No part of this publication may be reproduced, stored in a retrieval system, or transmitted in any form or by any means, electronic, mechanical, photocopying, recording, or otherwise, without written permission from the publisher.

First printing, September 2023

ISBN 978-88-544-2030-4
1 2 3 4 5 6   27 26 25 24 23

Printed and manufactured in Turkey by Arkadas Basim San Ltd Sti
Macun Mah.204 Cad. 141/3 Yenimahalle - 06374 Ankara